NAVAL REGULATIONS

ISSUED BY COMMAND

OF THE

PRESIDENT

OF THE

United States of America.

➤✳←

JANUARY 25, 1802.

Manufactured in the United States of America

CONTENTS.

—⊃✳︎⋐—

Of the duties of a commander in chief, or
 commander of a fquadron, - - - - - 1
Of the duties of a captain or commander, - 4
                a lieutenant, - - - - 13
                a failing-mafter, - - - 15
                a furgeon, - - - - - 16
                a chaplain, - - - - - 18
                a boatfwain and mafter fail-
                  maker, - - - - - ibid.
                a gunner, armorer, and gun-
                  fmith, - - - - - - 19
                a carpenter, - - - - 22
                a mafter-at-arms and corpo-
                  ral, · - - - - - 23
                midfhipmen, - - - - ibid.
                a cook, - - - - - - 24
Regulations to be obferved refpecting provifions, - - - - - - - - - - 25
              refpecting flops, - - - - 26
              refpecting the form and mode
                of keeping the log-book and
                journals, &c. - - - 28
              refpecting courts martial, - 34
              refpecting convoys, - - - 36

NAVAL REGULATIONS.

—➤✤€—

OF THE DUTIES OF A COMMANDER IN CHIEF, OR COMMANDER OF A SQUADRON.

1. HE is to inform the fecretary of the navy of all his proceedings which relate to the fervice.

2. He is to correfpond with the public offices, about fuch matters as relate to them, and fend to them an account of all directions given by him, which concern the faid offices.

3. He fhall inform himfelf of the properties of the veffels in his fquadron, that he may make ufe of them to advantage as occafion may require.

4. In order to facilitate the operations for which the fquadron is deftined, its commandant fhall take care to diftribute his orders to all the commanders under him, regulated by his inftructions from the fecretary of the navy.

5. Immediately on his receiving orders to fail, he fhall execute it as foon as the weather will

A

permit; and previous to his departure, he shall give an account to the secretary of the navy of the condition of his squadron, without omitting any essential circumstance.

6. He shall suit his sails according to the knowledge he ought to have of the qualities of the ships and circumstances of the weather, without obliging the heaviest sailors to an extraordinary exertion, from whence damage may result.

7. When the fleet shall be divided into squadrons or divisions, all the ships shall regulate their motions by those of their respective chiefs.

8. The commandant shall always maintain his squadron in a readiness to sail expeditiously; he shall from time to time visit the ships, as well to examine if they are in this due disposition, as to take care that they observe a good discipline.

9. He may suspend from their employs, the captains of vessels, or any other officers under his command, who, by their bad conduct, or other motives, he shall think deserving of such a punishment; but must immediately transmit an account thereof to the secretary of the navy, specifying his reasons for so doing, and furnish the captain or officer suspended, with a copy thereof.

10. The commandant of the squadron ought not to alter the appointments assigned to the officers, at the time of fitting out, without the weightiest and well founded reasons.

11. He is to preserve his instructions and particular orders, that he shall have received during the campaign, and other papers relative to his government, in the most intelligible disposition.

12. At the end of the cruise he shall transmit to the secretary of the navy a fair copy of

all his official correfpondence. He is to deliver to the fecretary of the navy the journal of his navigation, which he is to make during the cruife with the greateft exactnefs.

13. He is never to give orders to any captain to bear fupernumeraries, unlefs there be good caufe for it, which is to be expreffed in the body of the order; and he is to inform the fecretary of the navy when he gives fuch orders, and of his reafons for fo doing.

14. When he is at fea, he is frequently to exercife the fhips under his command, and draw them into lines of battle, when the weather is fair, and the fame can be done confiftently with his cruifing orders and without interruption to the voyage.

15. He is to vifit the fhips of his fquadron or divifion, and view the men on board, and fee them muftered, as often as he fhall think neceffary.

16. When he is in foreign parts, where naval or other officers are eftablifhed, he is to conform himfelf as much as poffible to the ftanding rules of the navy, in fuch directions as he fhall have occafion to give them; and never to put them under any extraordinary expenfes, unlefs the fervice fhould abfolutely require the fame.

17. He is never to intereft himfelf in the purchafe of any ftores or provifions in foreign parts, where there are proper officers appointed for that fervice; except there fhall be an abfolute neceffity to make ufe of his credit or authority, to procure fuch provifions or ftores as are wanted; but in that cafe, he fhall not be fo concerned as to have any private intereft in the fame.

OF THE DUTIES OF A CAPTAIN OR COMMANDER.

1. WHEN a captain or commander is appointed to command one of the United States ships, he is immediately to repair on board, and visit her throughout.

2. To give his constant attendance on board and quicken the dispatch of the work; and to send to the navy department weekly accounts, or oftener, if necessary, of the condition and circumstances she is in, and the progress made in fitting her out.

3. To take inventories of all the stores committed to the charge of his officers respectively, and to require from his boatswain, gunner, sailmaker, carpenter and purser, counterparts of their respective indents.

4. To cause his clerk to be present, and to take an account of all the stores and provisions that come on board, and when; which account he is to compare with the indents, in order to prevent any fraud or neglect.

5. To keep counter books of the expense of the ships stores and provisions, whereby to know the state and condition of the same; and to audit the accounts of the officers, entrusted therewith, once a week, in order to be a check upon them.

6. When ordered to recruit, he is to use his best endeavors to get the ship manned, and not to enter any but men of able bodies, and fit for service; he is to keep the established number of men complete, and not to exceed his complement.

7. When the ships company is completed, they shall be divided into messes and guards; and

he shall order without delay, the partition of the people for an engagement, to the end that, before they sail, every one may know his post.

8. He may grant to private ships of the nation the succours he lawfully may, taking from their captains or patrons a correspondent security, that the owners may satisfy the amount or value of the things supplied.

9. At all times, whether sailing alone or in a squadron, he shall have his ship ready for an immediate engagement: to which purpose, he shall not permit any thing to be on deck, that may embarrass the management of the guns, and not be readily cleared away.

10. As, from the beginning of the campaign, the plan of the combat ought to be formed, he shall have his directions given, and his people so placed, as not to be unprovided against any accident which may happen.

11. If it is determined to board the enemy, the captain is not under any pretext to quit his ship, whose preservation must be the chief object of his care; but he may appoint his second in command, or any other officer he thinks proper for the function, without attending to his antiquity.

12. He shall observe, during his cruise, the capacity, application, and behaviour of his officers; and for experience, he shall employ them in works and commissions that may manifest their intelligence.

13. He is to cause all new raised men and others, not skilled in seamanship, daily to lash up their hammocks, and carry them to the proper places for barricading the ship, whenever the weather

will permit ; and alfo to have them practifed in
going frequently every day, up and down the
fhrouds, and employed on all kinds of work, to
be created purpofely, to keep them in action,
and to teach them the duty of feamen.

14. To keep a regular mufter-book, fetting
down therein the names of all perfons entered
to ferve on board, with all circumftances relating to them.

15. Himfelf to mufter the fhip's company at
leaft once a week, in port, or at fea, and to be
very exact in this duty ; and if any perfon fhall
abfent himfelf from his duty, without leave, for
three fucceffive mufters, he is to be marked as a
run-away, on the fhips books.

16. To fend every month, one mufter-book
complete to the navy office, figned by himfelf
and purfer.

17. To make a lift of feamen run away, in-
ferting the fame at the end of the mufter-books,
and to diftinguifh the time, manner, and by
what opportunity they made their efcape : if the
defertion happens in any port of the United
States, he is to fend to the navy department their
names, place of abode, and all the circumftances
of their efcape.

18. The captain of the fhip fhall be refponfible for his crew, whofe defertion fhall be laid
to his charge, whenever it proceeds from a want
of neceffary care ; but if it proceeds from the
neglect of an officer who fhall have the charge
of a watering party, or any other duty on fhore,
and from his negligence any part of the crew
entrufted to him fhall defert, that officer fhall be
refponfible for the fame.

19. He is to make out tickets for all such sea-men as shall be discharged from his books, sign-ed by himself and purser, and to deliver them to none but the party; and if he be dead or absent he is to send the ticket forthwith to the navy-office.

20. He is not to suffer the ship's stores to be misapplied or wasted, and if such loss happens by the negligence or wilfulness of any of the ships company, he is to charge the value thereof against the wages of the offender on the muster and pay-books.

21. He shall make no alteration in any part of the ship.

22. He is to keep sentinels posted at the scut-tle, leading into all the store-rooms, and no per-son is to pass down but by leave from the cap-tain or commanding officer of the watch, which leave must be signified to the sentinel from the quarter deck.

23. He is to observe seasonable times in set-ting up his shrouds and other rigging, especially when they are new and apt to stretch; and also to favor his masts as much as possible.

24. He is to cause such stores as require it to be frequently surveyed and aired, and their de-fects repaired; and the store rooms to be kept airy and in good condition, and secured against rats.

25. He is not to make use of ships sails for covering boats, or for awnings.

26. The decks or gratings are not to be scrap-ed oftener than is necessary, but are to be wash-ed and swabbed once a day, and air let into the hold as often as may be.

27. He is to permit every officer to poſſeſs his proper cabin, and not to make any variation therein.

28. No perſon is to lie upon the orlop but by leave from the captain, nor to go among the cables with candles, but when ſervice requires it.

29. Such as ſmoke tobacco are to take it in the fore-caſtle, and in no other place without the captain's permiſſion, which is never to be given to ſmoke below the upper gun-deck.

30. Care is to be taken every night, on ſetting the watch, that all fire and candles be extinguiſhed, in the cock-room, hold, ſteward-room, cockpit, and every where between decks; nor are candles to be uſed in any other part of the ſhip but in lanterns, and that not without the captain's leave; and the lanterns muſt always be whole and unbroken.

31. He is not to ſuffer any perſon to ſuttle or ſell any ſorts of liquors to the ſhip's company, nor any debts for the ſame to be inſerted in the ſlop-book, on any pretence whatſoever.

32. Before the ſhip proceeds to ſea, he is, without any partiality or favor, to examine and rate the ſhips company, according to their abilities, and to take care that every perſon in the ſhip, without diſtinction, do actually perform the duty for which he is rated.

33. Before the ſhip ſails, he is to make a regulation for quartering the officers and men, and diſtributing them to the great guns, ſmall arms, rigging, &c. and a liſt of ſuch order and diſtribution is to be fixed up in the moſt public place of the ſhip. He is alſo frequently to exerciſe the ſhip's company in the uſe of the great guns

and ſmall arms; and to ſet down in his journal the times he exerciſes them.

34. The following number of men at leaſt, (excluſive of marines) are to be exerciſed and trained up to the uſe of ſmall arms, under the particular care of a lieutenant or maſter at arms.

44 gun ſhip - - - - - -	75 men.
36 do. - - - - - -	60 do.
32 do. - - - - - -	45 do.
24 and under 32 gun ſhips, -	40 do.
18 and under 24 do. - -	30 do.
All ſmaller veſſels, - - -	20 do.

35. If any officers are abſent from their duty when the ſhip is under ſailing orders, he is to ſend their names to the navy office with the cauſe of their abſence.

35. He is to take care of his boats, and ſecure them before blowing weather; alſo the colors are not to be kept abroad in windy weather, but due care taken of them.

36. He is not to carry any woman to ſea, without orders from the navy office, *or the commander of the ſquadron.*

37. When he is to ſail from port to port in time of war, or appearance thereof, he is to give notice to merchantmen bound his way, and take them under his care, if they are ready; but not to make unneceſſary ſtay, or deviate from his orders on that account.

38. He is to keep a regular journal, and at the end of every three months, he is to ſend a copy thereof to the navy office; and at the expiration of the voyage, to give in a general copy.

39. He is by all opportunities, to ſend an account of his proceedings to the navy office, with

the condition of the ship, men, &c. he is likewise to keep a punctual correspondence with every of the public offices, in whatsoever respectively concerns them.

40. He is not to go into any port, but such as are directed by his orders, unless necessitously obliged, and then not to make any unnecessary stay: if employed in cruising, he is to keep the sea the time required by his orders, or give reasons for acting to the contrary.

41. Upon all occasions of anchoring, he is to take great care in the choice of a good birth, and examine the quality of the ground for anchoring, where he is a stranger, sounding at least three cables lengths round the ship.

42. In foreign ports he is to use the utmost good husbandry in careening the ship, and not to do it but under an absolute necessity; none are to be employed in careening and refitting the ship but the ship's company, where it can be avoided; and for the encouragement of his own men, they are entitled to an extraordinary allowance per day; and to prevent any abuse herein, each ship has the number of operative men limited, as follows:

	In the United States.	In all foreign parts.
To master carpenters, carpenters' mates, shipwrights and caulkers, for working on board the ship they belong to, in caulking and fitting her for careen, and graving or tallowing her, per day,	50 cents.	75 cents.
For working on board any other of the United States' ships,	75 cents.	1 dollar.

And there fhall be allowed no more for cauïk-
ing a fhip, fitting her for careen, graving or tal-
lowing her, or other neceffary works, for each
careening or cleaning, than what amounts to the
labor of the following number of men for one
day, viz.

  For a 44—180 men for one day.
  For a 36—160 do.   do.
  For a 32—140 do.   do.
  For a 24— 90 do.   do.
  For an 18— 70 do.   do.
  All under— 30 do.   do.

43. If he is obliged to take up money abroad
for the ufe of the fhip, he is to negociate it at
the beft exchange.

44. He is to advife the proper officer of what
bills he draws, with the reafons thereof, and with
the faid bills fend duplicates of his accounts,
and vouchers for his difburfements, figned by
himfelf and purfer.

45. He is to take care that all ftores brought
on board be delivered to the proper officers; and
to take their receipts for the fame.

46. Upon the death of any officer he is to
take care that an inventory be taken of all his
goods and papers, and that the fame be fealed
up, and referved for the ufe of fuch as have a
legal right to demand them.

47. When any officer who has the cuftody of
ftores or provifions, fhall die, be removed or fuf-
pended, he is to caufe an exact furvey and inventory to be taken forthwith of the remains of
fuch ftores, which is to be figned by the fuccef-
for, who is to keep a duplicate thereof, and alfo
by the furveying officers.

48. Upon his own removal into another ship, he is to shew the originals of all such orders as have been sent to him and remain unexecuted, to his successor, and leave with him attested copies of the same.

49. He is to leave with his successor a complete muster-book, and send up all other books and accounts under his charge, to the officers they respectively relate to.

50. In case of shipwreck or other disaster, whereby the ship may perish, the officers and men are to stay with the remains as long as possible, and save all they can.

51. When any men borne for wages are discharged from one ship to another, the captain of the ship, from which they are so discharged, is to send immediately pay lists for such men to the navy office, and the purser of the ship from which they are so discharged, is also to supply the purser of the ship to which they are transferred, a pay list, stating the balances respectively due them.

52. To promote cleanliness and health, the following rules are to be attended to. 1. All men on board are to keep themselves in every respect as clean as possible. 2. That the ship be aired between decks as much as may be, and that she be always kept thoroughly clean. 3. That all necessary precautions be used, by placing sentinels or otherwise, to prevent people easing themselves in the hold, or throwing any thing there that may occasion nastiness. 4. That no fruit or strong liquors be sold on board the ship; *except in the judgment of the commander of the squadron, a limited quantity of fruit be necessary for the health of the crew, in which case he will issue an order*

53. He is refponfible for the whole conduct and good government of the fhip, and for the due execution of all regulations which concern the feveral duties of the officers and company of the fhip, who are to obey him in all things, which he fhall direct them for the fervice of the United States.

54. He is anfwerable for the faults of his clerk; nor can he receive his wages without the proper certificates, and muft make good all damages fuftained by his neglect or irregularity.

55. The quarter deck mu' never be left without one commiffioned office at leaft, *and the other neceffary officers which the captain may deem proper,* to attend to the duty of the fhip.

56. Commanding officers are to difcourage feamen from felling their wages; and not to atteft letters of attorney, if the fame appear granted in confideration of money given for the purchafe of wages.

—>✦<—

OF THE DUTIES OF A LIEUTENANT.

1. He fhall promptly, faithfully, and diligently, execute all fuch orders as he fhall receive from his commander, for the public fervice, nor abfent himfelf from the fhip without leave, on any pretence.

2. He is to keep a lift of the officers and men in his watch, mufter them, and report the names of the abfentees. He is to fee that good order be kept in his watch, that no fire or candle be burning, and that no tobacco be fmoked between decks.

B

3. He is not to change the courfe of the fhip at fea without the captain's directions, unlefs to prevent an immediate danger.

4. No boats are to come on board or go off without the lieutenant of the watch being acquainted with it.

5. He is to inform the captain of all irregularities, and to be upon deck in his watch, and prevent noife or confufion.

6. He is to fee that the men be in their proper quarters in time of action; and that they do perform all their duty.

7. He is to keep a journal, and, at the end of the voyage, to deliver a copy thereof into the navy-office.

8. The youngeft lieutenant is frequently to exercife the feamen in the ufe of fmall arms; and in the time of action he is to be chiefly with them.

9. He is to take great care of the fmall arms, and fee that they be kept clean and in good condition for fervice, and that they be not loft or embezzled.

10. The firft lieutenant is to make out a general alphabetical book of the fhip's company, and proper watch, quarter and ftation bills, in cafe of fire, manning of fhip, loofing and furling of fails, reefing of topfails at fea, working of fhip, mooring and unmooring, &c. leaving room for unavoidable alterations. This is to be hung in fome public part of the fhip, for the infpection of every perfon concerned.

11. No lieutenant or other officer belonging to a fhip of the United States to go on fhore, or on board another veffel, without firft obtaining

permiſſion from the captain or commanding officer, on his peril; and in the abſence of the captain, the commanding officer to grant no permiſſion of this ſort, without authority from the captain, previous to the captain's leaving the ſhip.

—⟶✦⟵—

OF THE DUTIES OF A SAILING-MASTER.

1. HE is to inſpect the proviſions and ſtores
ſent on board, and of what appears not good,
he is to acquaint the captain.

2. He is to take care of the ballaſt, and ſee
that it be clean and wholeſome, and ſign the
quantity delivered; and, in returning ballaſt, to
ſee that veſſels carry away their full lading.

3. He is to give his directions in ſtowing the
hold for the maſt-room, trimming the ſhip, and
for preſervation of the proviſions; and the oldeſt
proviſions to be ſtowed ſo as to be firſt expended.

4. He is to take ſpecial care that the rigging
and ſtores be duly preſerved; and to ſign the
carpenter's and boatſwain's expenſe-book, taking
care not to ſign undue allowances.

5. He is to navigate the ſhip, under the direction of his ſuperior officer, and ſee that the log
and log-book be duly kept, and to keep a good
look out.

6. He is duly to obſerve the appearances of
coaſts; and if he diſcovers any new ſhoals, or
rocks under water, to note them down in his
journal, with their bearing and depth of water.

7. He is to keep the hawſer clear when the
ſhip is at anchor, and ſee that ſhe is not girt
with her cables.

8. He is to provide himself with proper in-struments, and books of navigation, and keep a regular journal, noting therein the going out and coming in of all stores and provisions; and at the end of every cruise, deliver a copy thereof into the navy-office, with his log-book.

9. He is to be very careful not to sign any accounts, books, lists, or tickets, before he has thoroughly informed himself of the truth of every particular contained in the same.

10. He is to keep the ship in constant trim, and frequently to note her draught of water in the log-book. He is to observe the alterations made by taking in stores, water or ballast, and when the ship is in chase, or trying her sailing with another, he is to make memorandums of the draughts of water, the rake of the masts, state of the rigging, and to note every possible observation that may lead to the knowledge of the ship's best point of sailing.

—⋙✳⋘—

OF THE DUTIES OF A SURGEON.

1. TO inspect and take care of the necessaries sent on board for the use of the sick men; if not good, he must acquaint the captain; and he must see that they are duly served out for the relief of the sick.

2. To visit the men under his care twice a day, or oftener, if circumstances require it; he must see that his mates do their duty, so that none want due attendance and relief.

3. In cases that are difficult he is to advise with the surgeons of the squadron.

4. To inform the captain daily of the state of his patients.

5. When the sick are ordered to the hospitals, he is to send with them to the surgeon, an account of the time and manner of their being taken ill, and how they have been treated.

6. But none are to be sent to sick quarters, unless their distempers, or the number of the sick on board, are such, that they cannot be taken due care of; and this the surgeon is to certify under his hand, before removal. If the surgeon of the hospital finds they might have been cured in a little time on board, the surgeon of the ship is to have charged against his wages for every man so sent, ten dollars.

7. To be ready with his mates and assistants in an engagement, having all things at hand necessary for stopping of blood and dressing of wounds.

8. To keep a day-book of his practice, containing the names of his patients, their hurts, distempers, when taken ill, when recovered, removal, death, prescriptions, and method of treatment, while under cure.

9. From the last book he is to form two journals, one containing his physical, and the other his chirurgical practice; which are to be sent to the navy-office, at the end of every voyage.

10. Stores for the medical department are to be furnished upon his requisition, and he will be held responsible for the expenditure thereof.

11. He will keep a regular account of his receipts and expenditures of such stores, and transmit an account thereof to the accountant of the navy, at the end of every cruise.

OF THE DUTIES OF A CHAPLAIN.

1. HE is to read prayers at ſtated periods; per-form all funeral ceremonies over ſuch perſons as may die in the ſervice, in the veſſel to which he belongs; or, if directed by the commanding officer, over any perſon that may die in any other public veſſel.

2. He ſhall perform the duty of a ſchool-maſ-ter; and to that end he ſhall inſtruct the mid-ſhipmen and volunteers, in writing, arithmetic and navigation, and in whatſoever may contri-bute to render them proficients. He is likewiſe to teach the other youths of the ſhip, according to ſuch orders as he ſhall receive from the captain. He is to be diligent in his office, and ſuch as are idle muſt be repreſented to the captain, who ſhall take due notice thereof.

OF THE DUTIES OF A BOATSWAIN AND MASTER-SAIL-MAKER.

1. THE boatſwain is to receive into his charge, the rigging, cables, cordage, anchors, ſails, boats, &c.

2. He is not to cut up any cordage or canvaſs without an order in writing from the captain, and under the inſpection of the maſter; and al-ways to have by him a good quantity of ſmall plats for ſecurity of the cables.

3 He and his mates are to aſſiſt and relieve the watch, ſee that the men attend upon deck, and that the working of the ſhip be performed with as little confuſion as may be.

4. His accounts are to be audited and vouched by the captain and master, and transmitted to the navy-office.

5. If he has cause of complaint against any of the officers of the ship, with relation to the disposition of the stores under his charge, he is to represent the same to the navy-office, before the pay of the ship. He is not to receive his own wages until his accounts are passed.

6. He is not to sign any accounts, books, lists or tickets, before he has thoroughly informed himself of the truth of every particular therein contained.

7. *Master-Sail-maker.* He is, with his mate and crew, to examine all sails that are brought on board, and to attend all surveys and conversions of sails.

8. He is always and in due time to repair and keep the sails in order, fit for service.

9. He is to see that they are dry when put into the store-room, or very soon to have them taken up and aired, and see that they are secured from drips, damps and vermin, as much as possible.

10. When any sails are to be returned into store, he is to attend the delivery of them for their greater safety.

OF THE DUTIES OF A GUNNER, ARMORER, AND GUNSMITH.

1. The gunner is to receive by indenture, the ordnance, ammunition, small arms, and other stores allowed for the voyage; and if any part

thereof be not good, he is to reprefent the fame to the captain, in order to its being furveyed and returned.

2. He is to fee that the powder-room be well fecured, and in right order, before the powder is brought into the fhip.

3. Powder in the copper-hooped barrels to be lodged in the ground-tier; to fee that the doors of the powder-room be faft locked, the fkuttle well fhut and covered, and to deliver the keys to the captain.

4. He is timely to advife the captain when any powder comes on board, nor is he to remove it, prepare furzes, &c. without the captain's directions, fo that the fire and candles may be extinguifhed, fentinels pofted, and all care ufed to prevent accidents.

5. He is not to go or fend any one into the powder-rooms, but by leave of the captain, and to take care that they have nothing about them that will ftrike fire in falling.

6. No more than three rounds of parchment cartridges are to be filled at a time.

7. Perifhing ftores are to be furveyed and condemned; but if near any port in the United States, and they can conveniently be returned into ftore, they muft be, otherwife may be thrown over board.

8. Empty powder barrels are not be ftaved, but preferved, to fhift fuch as may be decayed.

9. *The Armorer and Gun-fmith,* Are to affift the gunner in the furvey and receipt of fmall arms, and to keep them clean and in good

order; but not to take them too often to pieces, which is detrimental to locks, &c.

10. Their station is in the gun-room, or such other place as the commanding officer may direct, where they are to observe the gunner's orders.

11. *The Gunner* is to receive the armorer's tools, and to account for them at the end of the voyage, in the same manner, as for the other stores under his charge.

12. In foreign parts, if the small arms want such repairs as cannot be done on board, the captain must cause a survey, and the defectives may be sent ashore to be repaired; but the armorer or gun-smith must attend to see the reparations well executed. They must return the small arms into store clean and in good order.

13. The quantities of powder for exercise, and on occasions of service and scaling, must be regulated by the captain or commanding officer. In time of action the allowance of powder must be reduced by degrees, until the same be lessened to one fourth of the weight of the shot. He is not to swab a gun when it grows hot, for fear of splitting.

14. He is to take care that the guns be placed upon their proper carriages; for, by this means, they will fit, and stand a proper height for the fill of the ports.

15. He is not to scale the guns oftener than the ship is refitted, unless upon extraordinary occasions, and with the captain's orders; and when they are loaded for service, he is to see them well tampioned and the vents filled with oakum.

16. He is to ufe great caution in order to pre-vent damage to fuch guns as are ftruck in the hold, by paying them all over with a coat of warm tar and tallow mixt, &c.

17. He is to take care of the ftores committed to him; for no wafte, that is not perifhable, will be allowed him, only reafonable wear; and if any accident, it muft be vouched by the captain.

18. He is to keep the boxes of grape-fhot and hand-grenadoes in a dry place.

19. He is not to load the guns with unfext mixtures, which greatly endanger their fplitting.

20. If he has caufe of complaint againft any of the officers of the fhip, with relation to the difpofition of the ftores under his charge, he is to reprefent the fame to the navy-office, before the pay of the fhip.

OF THE DUTIES OF A CARPENTER.

1. TO take upon him the care and prefervation of the fhip's hull, mafts, &c. and alfo the ftores committed to him by indenture.

2. To vifit and infpect all parts of the fhip daily, to fee that all things are well fecured and caulked, order the pumps and make reports to the captain.

3. In an engagement he is to be watchful, and have all materials ready to repair damages; and frequently to pafs up and down the hold with his crew, to be ready to plug up fhot-holes.

OF THE DUTIES OF A MASTER-AT-ARMS AND CORPORAL.

1. DAILY, by turns (as the captain shall appoint) to exercise the ship's company.

2. He is to place and relieve sentinels, to mount with the guard, and to see that the arms be kept in order.

3. He is to see that the fire and candles be put out in season, and according to the captain's order.

4. He is to visit all vessels coming to the ship, and prevent the seamen going from the ship, without leave.

5. He is to acquaint the officer of the watch with all irregularities in the ship which shall come to his knowledge.

6. *The corporals*, Are to act in subordination to the master-at-arms, and to perform the same duty under him, and to perform the duty themselves where a master-at-arms is not allowed.

—➤✳◀—

OF THE DUTIES OF MIDSHIPMEN.

1. NO particular duties can be assigned to this class of officers.

2. They are promptly and faithfully to execute all the orders for the public service, of their commanding officers.

3. The commanding officers, will consider the midshipmen, as a class of officers, meriting in an especial degree, the fostering care of their government. They will see therefore, that the

schoolmasters perform their duty towards them, by diligently and faithfully instructing them in those sciences appertaining to their department; that they use their utmost care, to render them proficients therein.

4. Midshipmen are to keep regular journals, and deliver them to the commanding officer at the stated periods, in due form.

5. They are to consider it as the duty they owe to their country, to employ a due portion of their time in the study of naval tactics, and in acquiring a thorough and extensive knowledge of all the various duties to be performed on board of a ship of war.

—➤✦◄—

OF THE DUTIES OF A COOK.

1. He is to have charge of the steep-tub, and is answerable for the meat put therein.

2. He is to see the meat duly watered, and the provisions carefully and cleanly boiled, and delivered to the men according to the practice of the navy.

3. In stormy weather he is to secure the steep-tub, that it may not be washed overboard; but if it should be inevitably lost, the captain must certify it, and he is to make oath to the number of pieces so lost, that it may be allowed in the purser's account.

—➤✦◄—

There shall be a distinct apartment appropriated on board of each vessel, for the surgeon, purser, boatswain, gunner, sail-maker, and carpenter, that they may keep the public goods committed respectively to their care.

REGULATIONS TO BE OBSERVED RESPECTING
PROVISIONS.

1. Provisions and slops are to be furnished upon the requisitions of the commanding officer,
founded upon the purser's indents.

2. The purser being held responsible for the
expenditure, shall, as far as may be practicable,
examine and inspect all provisions offered to the
vessel, and none shall be received that are object-
ed to by him, unless they are examined and ap-
proved of by at least two commissioned officers of
the vessel.

3. In all cases where it may appear to the purser, that provisions are damaged or spoiling, it
will be his duty to apply to the commanding officer, who will direct a survey, by three officers,
one of whom, at least, to be commissioned.

4. If upon a settlement of the purser's provision account, there shall appear a loss or deficiency of more than seven and a half per cent.
upon the amount of provisions received, he will
be charged with and held responsible for such
loss or deficiency exceeding the seven and a half
per cent. unless he shews by regular surveys that
the loss has been unavoidably sustained by damage or otherwise.

5. Captains may shorten the daily allowance
of provisions, when necessity shall require it,
taking due care that each man has credit for his
deficiency, that he may be paid for the same.

6. No officer is to have whole allowance while
the company is at short.

7. Beef for the use of the navy is to be cut
into 10 pound pieces, pork into 8 pound; and

C

every cafk to have the contents thereof marked on the head, and the perfon's name by whom the fame was furnifhed.

8. If there be a want of pork, the captain may order beef in the proportion eftablifhed, to be given out in lieu thereof, and vice verfa.

9. One half gallon of water at leaft fhall be allowed every man in foreign voyages, and fuch further quantity as fhall be thought neceffary on the home ftation, but on particular occafions the captain may fhorten this allowance.

10. To prevent the buying of cafks abroad, no cafks are to be fhipped which will want to be replaced by new ones before the veffel's return to the United States.

11. If any provifions flip out of the flings, or are damaged through carelefnefs, the captain is to charge the value againft the wages of the offender.

12. Every fhip to be provided with a feine, and the crew fupplied with frefh provifions as it can conveniently be done.

—❧✠❧—

REGULATIONS RESPECTING SLOPS.

1. Slop clothing is to be charged to the purfer at the coft and charges, and he is to be held accountable for the expenditure.

2. And in no cafe will the purfer be credited even for any alledged lofs by damage in flops, unlefs he fhews by regular furveys figned by three officers, one of whom at leaft to be commiffioned, that the lofs has been unavoidably fuftained

by *damage*, and not by any neglect or inatten-
tion on his part.

3. And as a compenfation for the rifque and
refponfibility, the purfer fhall be authorized to
difpofe of the flops to the crew at a profit of 10
per cent. ; but he muft at the end of every cruife
render a regular and particular flop account,
fhewing by appropriate columns, the quantities
of each feveral kinds of articles received or pur-
chafed, and the prices and amount, and from
whom, when and where, and he fhall fhew the
quantities difpofed of, and to whom, and at what
prices ; fo that his flop account will fhew the
articles, prices and amount received and difpofed
of.

4. On the death or removal of a purfer, the
commanding officer will caufe a regular furvey
to be made on the flops remaining on hand, and
an inventory thereof to be made out and figned
by at leaft two commiffioned officers.

5. Seamen deftitute of neceffaries may be fupplied with flops by an order from the captain,
after the veffel has commenced her voyage.

6. None are to receive a fecond fupply until
they have ferved full two months, and then not
exceeding half their pay, and in the fame proportion for every two months if they fhall be in
want.

7. Slops are to be iffued out publicly and in
the prefence of an officer, who is to be appointed by the captain, to fee the articles delivered to
the feamen and others, and the receipts given for
the fame, which he is alfo to certify.

8. The captain is to oblige thofe who are rag-
ged or want bedding, to receive fuch neceffaries
as they ftand in need of.

9. The captain is to sign the slop-book before the ship is paid off, or on his removal from the ship at any time, the purser is to send the same to the proper accounting officer duly signed.

10. On the discharge of a man by ticket, the value of the clothes he has been supplied with must be noted on the same in words at length.

11. If necessity requires the buying of clothes in foreign parts, the captain must cause them to be procured of the kinds prescribed for the navy, and as moderate as possible: he must also, by the first opportunity, cause an invoice of the same to be forwarded to the navy department.

REGULATIONS RESPECTING THE FORM AND MODE OF KEEPING THE LOG-BOOK AND JOURNALS ON BOARD OF SHIPS OR OTHER VESSELS OF THE UNITED STATES.

For the purpose of establishing uniformity, the President orders as follows, viz.

1. The quarter bill, log-tables or book, and journals of the officers, must be kept conformably to the annexed models.

2. The captains or commanders will cause to be laid before them the first and fifteenth of every month, the journals of the sea lieutenants, masters, midshipmen, and volunteers under their orders, will examine and compare them with their own, and will send them at the end of every cruise or expedition to the navy department.

3. If any of the said journals contain observations or remarks which may contribute to the improvement of geography, by ascertaining the lati-

tude and longitude, fixing, or rectifying the position of places, the heights and views of land, charts, plans or descriptions of any port, anchorage ground, coasts, islands or danger little known; remarks relative to the direction and effects of currents, tides or winds; the officers or persons appointed to examine them, will make extracts of whatever appears to merit to be preserved, and after these extracts have been communicated to the officer or author of the journal from which they have been drawn, and that he has certified in writing to the fidelity of his journal, as well as of the charts, plans and views, which he has joined to it, the same shall be signed by the officers and examiners, and transmitted with their opinion thereon to the secretary of the navy, to be preserved in the depot of charts, plans and journals.

MODEL OF A JOURNAL, kept o
of   guns

H	K	F	Courfes	Winds.	Occurrences, remarks and hiftor of guns Ce
1					
2					
3					
4					
5					
6					
7					
8					
9					
10					
11					
12					
1					
2					
3					
4					
5					
6					
7					
8					
9					
10					
11					Diftance per Log—
12					

oard the United States.
ommander, by

ents, &c made on board the United States ander, on the day of year	Refult of Day's work.
	Courfe made good.
	Diſtance.
	Diff latt'de·
	Departure.
	Mer'd diſtance.
	DD long'de.
	Long'de ob'd.
	Latt'de ob'd.
	Var'n pr amp'de
	Var'n pr. azim'th.
	Current.

MODEL OF A LOG-BOOK, kept
  of   guns,   Co

H	K	F	Courses	Winds.	Occurrences and remarks, on bo of guns Co
1					
2					
3					
4					
5					
6					
7					
8					
9					
10					
11					
12					
1					
2					
3					
4					
5					
6					
7					
8					
9					
10					
11					Diftance per Log→
12					

ard the United States
ander, by   Sailing Mafter.

United States Frigate			
nder, on	the	day of	year

Latt'de. Obf'd
Long'de. Obf'd
Vari. Even'g. Amp'de·
Vari. Morn'g. Amp'de.

REGULATIONS RESPECTING COURTS MARTIAL.

1. All courts martial are to be held, offences tried, fentences pronounced, and execution of fuch fentences done, agreeably to the articles and orders contained in an act of Congrefs, made on the 23d of April, in the year 1800, entitled "an act for the better government of the navy of the United States."

2. Courts martial may be convened as often as the Prefident of the United States, the fecretary of the navy, or commander in chief of a fleet, or commander of a fquadron, while acting out of the United States, fhall deem it neceffary.

3. All complaints are to be made in writing, in which are to be fet forth the facts, time, place, and the manner how they were committed.

4. The judge advocate is to examine witneffes upon oath, and by order of the commander in chief, or in his abfence, of the prefident of the court, to fend an attefted copy of the charge to the party accufed, in time to admit his preparing his defence.

5. In all cafes, the youngeft member muft vote firft, and fo proceed up to the prefident.

—⤜✣⤛—

REGULATIONS RESPECTING CONVOYS.

1. A commander of a fquadron or commander of a fhip appointed to convoy the trade of the United States, muft give neceffary and proper inftructions in writing, and figned by him.

felf, to all the mafters of merchant fhips and veffels under his protection.

2. He is to take an exact lift in proper form,
containing the names of all the fhips and veffels
under his convoy and fend a copy thereof to the
navy department, before he fails.

3. He is not in time of actual war to chafe
out of fight of his convoy, but be watchful to
defend them from attack or furprife ; and if dif-
treffed, to afford them all neceffary affiftance.—
He is to extend the fame protection to his convoy, when the United States are not engaged in
war.

4. If the mafter of a fhip fhall mifbehave, by
delaying the convoy, abandoning, or difobeying
the eftablifhed inftructions, the commander is
to report him with a narrative of the facts to the
fecretary of the navy, by the firft opportunity.

5. The commander is to carry a top-light in
the night, to prevent feparation, unlefs on particular occafions, he may deem it improper.

6. He may order his fignals to be repeated by
as many fhips of war under his command, as he
may think fit.

7. When different convoys fet fail at the fame
time, or join at fea, they are to keep together,
fo long as their courfes lie together : when it thus
happens, the eldeft commander of a convoy,
fhall command in the firft poft ; the next eldeft
in the fecond, and fo on according to feniority.

8. Commanders of different convoys are to
wear the lights of their refpective pofts, and
repeat the fignals, in order, as is ufual to flag
officers.

9. Convoys are to sail like divisions, and proper signals to be made at separation.

—❧✦❧—

The President of the United States of America, ordains and directs the commanders of squadrons, and all captains and other officers in the navy of the United States, to execute, and cause to be executed, the aforesaid regulations.

By command,

R Smith

Secretary of the Navy.

NOTES ON EARLY
NAVAL REGULATIONS

—➤✦⇐—

THIS is a facsimile copy of a book which saw service with the Mediterranean Squadron of the U. S. Navy in the Barbary Wars. It was the personal copy of Commodore Edward Preble, brilliant naval leader and hero of the blockade and bombardment of Tripoli, 1803–1804. This little volume embodies the codified, printed executive regulations which governed the U. S. Navy at that time. Other regulations, the ones with teeth in them—the laws of Congress that provided penalties for mutiny, cowardice, murder, desertion, theft, and like crimes—were also very much in effect. Both sets of regulations, congressional and presidential, were derived from the naval laws, regulations, and customs of England. Beyond this simple statement of ancestry extends the long and interesting history of naval regulations, one chapter of which is the story of the *Naval Regulations* of 1802.

On November 28, 1775, the Continental Congress adopted a code of naval regulations which was prepared by John Adams and six members of the colonial Naval Committee. Copies of their *Rules for the Regulation of the Navy of the United Colonies of North America*... were hastily printed and distributed before the year was out. A British naval officer of the day would have recognized the *Rules* to be a shortened list of articles, some taken verbatim, from the Parliamentary laws relating to the government of His Majesty's ships, vessels, and forces by sea (consolidated into one Act in 1749), and from the Lords Commissioners of the Admiralty's *Regulations and Instructions Relating to His Majesty's Service at Sea.*

These rules of the United Colonies saw our Navy through the Revolutionary War and were readopted as law under the Constitution. However, along with the preparations for the imminent war at sea with France, consideration was given to revising them. On November 29, 1798, Secretary of the Navy Benjamin Stoddert wrote to Captain John Barry, suggesting that inasmuch as he and Captains Truxtun, Dale, Decatur, and Tingey were in Philadelphia, "it would be useful and important" if they would consider altering "the extremely defective" regulations. The rules so revised were passed by Congress, March 2, 1799 as An Act for the Government of the Navy of the United States, and again revised and passed a year later as An Act for the Better Government of the Navy of the United States.

Not much was changed either in wording or content from the colonial rules. The articles in these acts were concerned mostly with offenses committed on shipboard and provisions for their punishment, procedures for courts martial, the distribution of prize money, and other laws not new to the service. These then were the Articles of War or Articles for the Government of the Navy and have constituted, with changes over the years, the naval code up to our own time. Concurrent with these laws were instructions, orders, circulars, and regulations emanating from the President or Secretary of the Navy directed to ship captains and other officers.

In an interesting document addressed to his crew concerning mutinous assemblies aboard the frigate *Constellation* in 1798, Captain Thomas Truxtun cited both the legislative and executive regulations: "That in Case I ever hear of a Murmur in the Ship, or any Expressions, that have a Tendency to disorganize, or cause Disorder, or Discontent in any Way whatever, or of any Threats, I am determined to put the following Article of War in Execution, and comply strictly with the Orders of the President of the United States." He then quoted the article of the re-adopted colonial rules which provided death, "or such other Punishment, as a Court Martial shall direct," for beginning, exciting, causing or joining any mutiny. He next listed Articles 23, 48, 68, and 85 of "The Order of the President of the United States under the Head of Regulations respecting the Duties of Officers at Sea." These articles were among the one hundred and sixteen regulations for officers which made up a part of the *Marine Rules and Regulations* of President John Adams, issued in 1798. The four articles mentioned do not appear as such in the 1802 *Naval Regulations,* although another Adams article (which Truxtun cited as Article 5, respecting provision of water) does appear verbatim as Article 9, page 26.

Each captain also had his own set of rules and

regulations for the operation of his ship and the conduct of the crew. These internal regulations were quite explicit. Commodore Preble posted a list of more than one hundred general rules, along with a special set for the master and purser, on board his flagship *Constitution* in 1803–1804. Routines pertaining to the heaving of the log, the sounding of the hold, the serving of meals, etc., were listed in detail, and requirements such as, "Every seaman belonging to the ship is expected to supply himself with the following . . . cloaths," were stated. Another list of twenty-four regulations also survives from the *Congress,* dated 1800. Captain Truxtun, aboard the *Constellation* in 1798, had so many printed instructions that one of his officers complained that it would take an attorney to learn and remember them all. Some concern for the uniformity of rules is evident in a section of the Act for the Government of the Navy of 1799 which provided that no rules were to be made by commanders at variance with the act, and that in making private rules and regulations they were to " . . . keep in view also the custom and usage of the sea-service most common to our nation."

At the beginning of Thomas Jefferson's administration a new set of presidential regulations was proposed. His Secretary of the Navy, Robert Smith, on March 13, 1801, wrote to Captain John Barry requesting him to examine an enclosed " . . . sketch of the rules and regulations for the Government of the officers of the navy," with a view to making remarks and additions concerning them. Barry was then to forward the enclosure to Captain Truxtun for his improvements, and he in turn was to send it on to Captain Richard V. Morris. Morris was to send it to Captain Alexander Murray, who would return it to the Secretary, with the collective comments that were to have been made on the blank paper attached to the "sketch." The resulting printed *Naval Regulations,* dated January 25, 1802, were again a reworking of existing Adams presidential regulations and the British naval *Regulations and Instructions.*

These rules as reviewed by the four experienced naval captains were printed by one of the several printers who had recently moved from Philadelphia to the federal city or to Georgetown, in order to be near the new seat of government. Here the 1802 *Naval Regulations* appeared without imprint, duodecimo in collation, and probably in plain paper wrappers. The Secretary of the Navy's correspondence does not help in finding the name of the printer of the regulations, although his principal clerk did write to at least two District printers in late 1801 on other matters. Apparently no records concerning payment for this printing job remain, either. Typographic evidence, however, indicates that the firm of Way & Groff, of North E Street, Washington, probably did the printing.

The month of February, 1802, found Secretary Robert Smith distributing fifty copies each of the *Naval Regulations* to the several ships fitting out for the Barbary campaigns and to the squadron already in the Mediterranean Sea. Letters were addressed to Commodore Truxtun of the *Chesapeake,* at Norfolk; Captain Murray, *Constellation,* Philadelphia; Captain Preble, *Adams,* New York; Captain Morris, *Constitution,* Boston; and to Commodore Dale on the Mediterranean Station. Also, twenty copies were to be sent to Lt. Andrew W. Sterrett of the *Enterprise,* at Baltimore. Smith ordered that these commanders were to receive the *Naval Regulations* and were to distribute them among their officers, "enjoining them the strictest attention thereto." Copies were probably also distributed on an individual basis, for on February 26th Midshipman William S. Butler in Pittsburgh was sent one along with his orders to report to the frigate *Constitution* at Boston.

If Thomas Jefferson, by whose presidential command the *Navy Regulations* was issued, ever owned a copy, it was not among his books sold to Congress in 1815, although the Way & Groff printing of the *Rules and Articles for the Better Government of the Troops,* Washington, 1800, was part of his library. Captain Preble's copy remained in his family and is now owned by his last descendant, Rear Admiral Dundas Preble Tucker, U. S. Navy Retired. This copy and one that belonged to Thomas Truxtun, which the U. S. Naval Academy Library acquired in 1860, are similarly bound in leather and interleaved with blank pages.

The story of the 1802 *Naval Regulations* ends with the promulgation of the next of a long succession of editions of regulations in 1818; but the book itself remains to tell of certain aspects of life at sea during the historic days in which some of our finest naval traditions were established.

H. R. Skallerup,
Associate Professor
United States Naval Academy.
Annapolis, Maryland

January 1970

A facsimile reprint of the 1775 colonial *Rules* was published in 1944 by the Naval Historical Foundation, Washington, as its Reprint Series I, no. 1. It contains two pages of introductory matter, and eight pages of facsimile.

The *Marine Rules and Regulations* of President Adams was printed in Philadelphia by John Fenno in 1798 (Evans, # 34893). The last page [57] is signed by Secretary of War, James McHenry. It contains several sections of regulations in addition to those on the duties of officers. A reprint of it, dated 1799, also exists (Evans, # 36544).

In 1809, and again in 1814, slightly revised editions of the 1802 *Naval Regulations* appeared with "Washington City, Printed for the Navy Office," in their imprints. These editions were signed by Navy Secretaries Paul Hamilton and B. W. Crowninshield, respectively.

Sources used for these Notes include [v. 1–2, 5] of *Naval Documents Related to the Quasi-War Between the United States and France* (¶ 3, 5–6 above) ; [v. 3] of *Naval Documents Related to the United States Wars with the Barbary Powers* (¶ 6) ; Record Group 45 of the U. S. National Archives: "Letters to Officers, Ships of War" (¶ 7, 9) ; and "Miscellaneous Letters Sent by the Secretary of the Navy" (¶ 8).

A general discussion of the regulations, 1775–1941, appeared in the *Proceedings of the U. S. Naval Institute*, v. 73, p. 1354–1361 (Nov., 1947) : "A History of Regulations in the U. S. Navy," by L. H. Bolander. Details on the origins of the British and colonial regulations were also given in the *Proceedings*, v. 45, p. 355–376 (Mar., 1919) : "On the History of Discipline in the Navy," by C. R. Williams. James Snedeker's, *A Brief History of Courts-Martial*, published by the U. S. Naval Institute, 1954, brings the history of naval regulations up to the enactment of the Uniform Code of Military Justice in 1950.

A Note About This Edition

Printed on 75 lb. Curtis Rag Laid in
two-color offset by
Collins Lithographing and Printing Co., Inc.
Baltimore, Maryland
Bound by A. Horowitz & Son,
Clifton, New Jersey

Design by Harvey Satenstein